Mister Mustache Books LLC™

Proudly Presents

Joyful Tails

in Concert with

Angels to the Animals
Blazin' Trails Bottle Babies
Cats of Davidson
Killer Kitties Rescue 2.0
Miles to Go Kitten Rehab
Save the Clefts Rescue
Sunkissed Acres NC Rescue
Three Brothers Animal Rescue

Compiled and Edited by Catherine A. Thornton | Illustrated by Elizabeth L. Haskins

As attributed to Mahatma Gandhi, "The true measure of any society can be found in how it treats its most vulnerable members." The conviction may not have been intended to apply to animals, but it fits. Therefore, this compendium of real-life stories of animals, abandoned or born to unforgiving circumstances not of their making or choice, is dedicated to those awe-inspiring human beings who feel the pain of those vulnerable animals and choose not to turn away from their discomfort, but, rather, to heal their suffering. Whether they do so as part of an organization or on their own, as concerned and caring citizens, they are our better angels. They are the ones by whom society could be measured as exceptional. I only wish there were more of them and that the personal cost they bear for caring (the physical, mental, and financial tolls) were not so steep. I ask you to appreciate and support them, for they need and deserve that. These angels among us may not have wings to fly, but they have heart, determination, and strength in extraordinary measure.

— Cathy Thornton

Mister Mustache Books LLC™

ISBN No. 979-8-9937565-4-7

First paperback edition printed in February 2026 by IngramSpark in the United States of America.

Illustrations by Elizabeth L. Haskins

www.mrmustachebooks.com

Letter from the Editor

Dearest Reader:

cccccbhdieucnhktbeubbhektkuflnbkcjtvkhccgejf* ... oops, one of my cats says "hello." Liz would tell you she is a frequent recipient of such communiques whenever I forget to lock my computer.

I was going to say first and foremost, but now second and foremost, thank you for purchasing this book. The individuals who formed and operate the rescues you will be reading about are truly amazing people. I wanted to pay homage to them for their contributions to our communities by compiling just a few of their stories in book form. This is a very personal and heartfelt endeavor for me and Liz, as we know these people. We have adopted from them, fostered for them, and donate to their causes.

My own family has rescued and found loving forever homes for more than 200 cats and kittens in a decade since moving to North Carolina. While I believe the public is supportive of animal rescue, I don't think most people realize the amount of work, mental anguish, and financial cost involved. These rescues are small organizations, trying only to cover their costs as nonprofits and never fully doing so. If an animal in its care needs something and the rescue lacks the funds to cover that item, the individual operating the rescue expends personal resources to ensure the animals never go without. It is messy, exhausting, expensive, heartbreaking, and sometimes frustrating, but it is also one of the most rewarding things one can imagine. Seeing photos and videos of happy, loving pets, who, when first encountered, were sick or starving or injured and always frightened little creatures, gives all of us who rescue more joy than words can adequately express. It is why I titled this book "Joyful Tails." It's what animal rescue is all about.

I have held and comforted kittens as they've taken their last breaths, crying over the chance they never got (sometimes not even the chance to open their eyes and see the world around them). I have laughed. Such as when we took in a large and very rotund cat we were told was heavily pregnant, only to quickly discover it was just a big fat neutered male. I have marveled at the unlikely rescue of a kitten who escaped her carrier at the vet, survived crossing a four-lane highway, was helped by a series of wonderful human beings, and eventually made her way into our home. Penny is now the beloved pet of my former boss and living her best life in Virginia. I guarantee that every person in animal rescue could share story after story of triumphs and defeats. This book shares just a fraction of those stories, but I hope you read them and feel all the love that went into the animals saved and that you gain a newfound appreciation for (and eagerness to assist) the causes championed by these inspiring groups.

Again, thank you for your support. It means more than you know.

*Actual cat-generated correspondence

Contents

About the Rescue

Angels to the Animals is a 501(c)(3) nonprofit organization based out of Denver, North Carolina.

The rescue is committed to encouraging and educating owners about creating a nurturing and humane environment for their pets, as well as finding loving, permanent homes for surrendered pets.

Its mission is to protect and advocate for pets in need and to build a humane community that promotes compassion, kindness, and a clear opportunity for quality life beyond chained, forgotten, and neglected animals in Lincoln County, North Carolina.

Angels to the Animals' team of volunteers provides frequent and consistent on-site care, including food and water, shelter and straw, proper veterinary care including vaccinations, flea and tick control, heartworm testing and treatment, and spay and neuter, as well as toys and treats.

And of course, all of this is accompanied by lots of love.

How to Contact and How to Help

E-mail the rescue at: info@angelstotheanimals.org

Angels to the Animals appreciates any denomination of financial support. Whether you'd like to make a one-time financial contribution, set up a monthly or quarterly financial donation, or donate a wish-list item, the rescue is grateful for your generosity.

Donate to the rescue by visiting: https://angelstotheanimals.org/donate

On the Angels to the Animals web site, as listed above, you will find links to make a financial donation by mail or online via PayPal or Venmo. You will also find links to the rescue's Amazon and Chewy wish lists, should you prefer to lend your support in that way.

View the rescue's adoptable pets at:

https://www.petfinder.com/member/us/nc/denver/angels-to-the-animals-nc1230/

Meet Lucky ♥

Angels to the Animals thinks Lucky may have been cared for in his very early days but was then given to his first owner's parents and left to live outside on a chain for years. He was extremely neglected, a horrible way for any noble animal to exist.

At long last another member of the family, concerned for Lucky's well-being, contacted Angels to the Animals to see if the rescue could find Lucky a better living situation—assuming the parents could be convinced to surrender him. Fortunately, they did.

Lucky was a bit older when he came to the rescue, was a pitbull without manners, and was not good with other dogs or cats, giving Angels to the Animals a difficult rehoming task. On top of that, Lucky tested positive for heartworms and had to undergo a long, difficult, and painful treatment to rid his body of the worms that were slowly killing him.

Lucky moved among several foster homes in that period, as no one could keep him long term. He eventually had to enter a boarding facility when no foster was available and no adoption prospects were in sight at the time. The

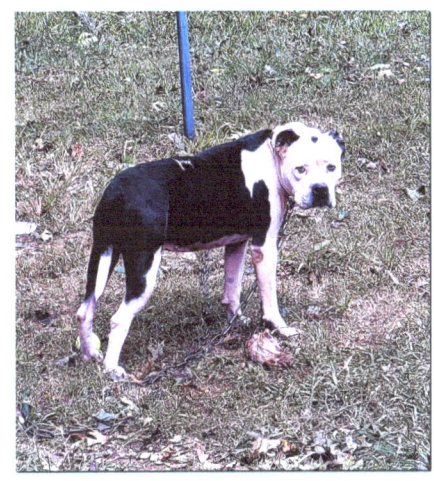

Above and below, Lucky lived an unlucky life for years, left outdoors on a chain to languish in the elements. Luckily, his life began to change once Angels to the Animals rescued him from that heartbreaking existence.

rescue was heartbroken about this; and sadly, Lucky remained in boarding for months until his lucky day finally arrived.

Now, thanks to a remarkable mom and dad, Lucky finally enjoys the best life! He has discovered the joys of being on a boat, riding in a golf cart, and walks along the beach, as well as the simple pleasure of being in his dad's truck with his head out the window.

It took a long time to get there, but Lucky's tale is one of Angels to the Animals' most cherished success stories. Today, Lucky is a lucky boy indeed!

Clockwise from the top, Lucky, on the "high seas"; looking utterly adorable riding a golf cart and sporting a rather debonair cap; at the beach, enjoying the sand and water beneath his paws; and finally, overjoyed about an outing in his dad's truck.

Meet Frankie

Frankie came to Angels to the Animals as a four-month-old puppy weighing just over seven pounds and extremely weak and emaciated. He was in a coma upon arrival at the emergency hospital, and tests showed numerous hookworms (far too many to count). The vet indicated Frankie should have weighed three times what he did!

Above, no living creature deserves to suffer this way. Below, that face and those ears! Need we say more?! At bottom, best friends are the best!

He was in and out of the hospital for several nights, struggling to overcome severe diarrhea as a result of the massive parasite load borne by his little body. He finally began to improve, but it was a long process to heal him; and it was during this time the rescue realized Frankie was also deaf!

After one false start with a "foster-to-adopt" trial, Frankie went to a new foster. Once again, the rescue was on the search for this sweet pup's "happy ever after." Finding a home for a deaf dog was new to the group; and sadly, there was not a lot of interest.

Then one night, Frankie attended a "Dog Night at the Ballpark" baseball game with his new foster parents, sporting his "adopt me" vest. A family observed him, was smitten, and was undeterred by his disability. A "meet and greet" was scheduled with the family's blue heeler, and the two dogs hit it off right away! Frankie was quickly adopted and is now loving life in his loving forever home!

Meet Danny ♥

Angels to the Animals was contacted when someone found a puppy, only eight weeks old, with a mangled leg. It is unknown whether he'd been hit by a car or abused. The rescue rushed the young puppy to the vet, where it was determined his leg could not be saved. Amputation was necessary. While Danny's surgery proceeded, the rescue searched, without success, for an owner, ultimately assuming responsibility for him the next day.

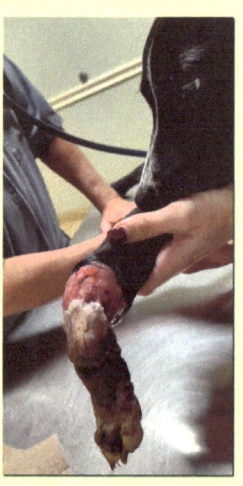

Above, a difficult sight. Danny was surely in agony.

To the rescue's surprise, this brave little one acted like he'd never lost a limb at all. (Front amputations are typically more difficult on dogs, as most of their weight is carried at the front of their bodies.) Danny adapted effortlessly to his new reality.

Danny adored other dogs and, once healed, could play and romp with the best of them. He was, however, guarded with humans, especially men. Therefore, after several fosters and a failed adoption, the rescue enrolled Danny in an eight-week-long boarding and training program at which he excelled. The next hard part was finding an adopter willing to take on a tripod and dedicate time to work with him on his quirks.

Above, Danny, recovered (perhaps catching a game on TV?). At left, with his forever person.

Angels to the Animals was blessed to find just that for Danny! This special pup now has a wonderful human dad; and they are, indeed, a match made in heaven!

Meet Isabella ♥

When Angels to the Animals says "animals," it truly means ALL animals. A property at which the rescue was caring for dogs also had a pig without so much as a name. The rescue named her Isabella (Izzy, for short). The poor girl was neglected, not fed or cared for properly, and living in a pen out of which she couldn't even see. It was a depressing and lonely life, so devastating for such an intelligent, gentle soul.

Above, Izzy's pen was no place for such a wonderful creature. Below, Isabella is thriving at Harley June, with companion animals and superb care.

The rescue brought Izzy fruits and vegetables whenever it visited and was finally successful in convincing Izzy's owner to let the group find her a new home. It reached out to Harley June Farm and Sanctuary in Morganton, North Carolina. Not only did Harley June agree to help, but farm staff even traveled down to pick her up.

Angels to the Animals volunteers accompanied farm staff on the return trip, excited to see the place that would now be Isabella's home. The rescue was so impressed and thrilled with Isabella's new "digs," everyone was overcome with joy!

To this day, the rescue receives updates on Izzy and is always delighted to hear how much she is loving farm life and her numerous friends. Thankfully, darling Isabella is now the joyful one!

Meet Red, Maggie, and Thor ♥

Red, Maggie, and Thor were found on a vacant lot together, each tied to a tree in the middle of winter without adequate shelter. They had nothing in their doghouses to keep them warm. Their owner would come by once a week, late at night, and leave food for them that never lasted long enough; and he never changed their water. To make things worse, the owner would go to the back of the property and shoot off his gun at midnight, terrifying and traumatizing the dogs.

Angels to the Animals stepped in when a worried neighbor alerted the group. Seeing the heavy chains on these dogs and the fear and sadness in their eyes was among the most devastating things one can imagine. It shook everyone involved in saving these helpless, blameless animals to the core. The rescue believes the dogs were involved in some sort of fighting enterprise, but it was never proven.

Angels to the Animals initially cared for Red, Maggie, and Thor on site, bringing them straw,

At right, from top to bottom, Red, Maggie, and Thor had heavy chains around their necks and desolation in their eyes.

food, and fresh water and showing them the love they'd never experienced but so very much deserved.

One might expect these dogs to have been mean or aggressive, yet they they were the complete opposite of that. They craved love and attention, human touch, and kindness.

Angels to the Animals contacted animal control, and the owner eventually surrendered the dogs to the rescue. They were all placed into foster homes where they healed with time, both physically and emotionally, from their ghastly ordeal.

Red, Maggie, and Thor have since all found wonderful, loving families who adore and spoil them just as these amazing animals always should have been treated. Thanks to their human angels, today their eyes are only alight with joy and love.

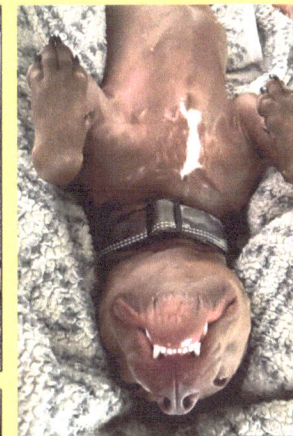

Above left, the gentle Thor with his new best friend. To the left and above right, Red embodies peace and a quiet joy in his forever home, exactly where he was always meant to be. Below, Maggie, outdoors for all the right reasons and enjoying a nap with her bestie.

Our Mission and Our Marvels in Pictures

About the Rescue

Blazin' Trails Bottle Babies is a 501(c)(3) nonprofit caring for fragile, at-risk puppies who need immediate, intensive care. The rescue was established in 2024 after its founder, scrolling on social media, came across a post about a newborn puppy who was just 1 day old and missing a front leg, as you'll read about in Blaze's story that follows.

With no experience bottle feeding puppies but possessing a medical background, his new "mom" wanted to help. While vet after vet advised euthanasia, uncomfortable treating such a small, vulnerable puppy, Blazin' Trails' founder wasn't ready to give up. Diving into research, she was determined to learn everything possible to care for this tiny life.

What she discovered was a lack of reliable information—no solid guidance or expert advice tailored to neonatal puppies. That's when she realized something better had to be built. With the support of a dedicated team, she began to gather the knowledge and resources needed to save these fragile babies. Together, they established a foundation of specialized care, so puppies like Blaze would have a real chance at life.

About the Rescue, Continued

Fast forward to today. Since opening its doors just 2 short years ago, Blazin' Trails has proudly saved the lives of more than 250 precious pups.

How to Contact and How to Help

E-mail the rescue at: info@blazintrailsbottlebabies.org

Every puppy Blazin' Trails saves starts with someone like you choosing to help. Your support keeps incubators warm, bottles full, and tiny fighters safe while they heal and grow. Here are the easiest ways to give:

Zelle (the rescue's favorite way to receive donations)
Send directly to info@blazintrailsbottlebabies.org (Zelle lets more of your gift go straight to the puppies, with no fees)

Amazon Wish List: https://a.co/j2lzN4D

Online donation form: Prefer to give by card? You can make a secure, one-time or monthly gift using the donation form on this page: https://blazintrailsbottlebabies.org/donate/.

No matter how you choose to give, you are helping orphaned newborn puppies gain a second chance at life, love, and a forever home.
Blazin' Trails Bottle Babies thanks you for being part of their story.

Meet Isaiah

Isaiah, a pitbull mix, was born with hydrocephalus, the result of irresponsible overbreeding.

Hydrocephalus is informally known as "water on the brain," and it is deadly if left untreated. It is the reason for Isaiah's dome-shaped head and the downcast, almost sad appearance of his eyes. It can also cause poor coordination, seizures, and even behavorial issues due to pressure on the brain.

Little Isaiah is blind and deaf as the result of his condition, but he has learned to sit and adores playing like any other young dog.

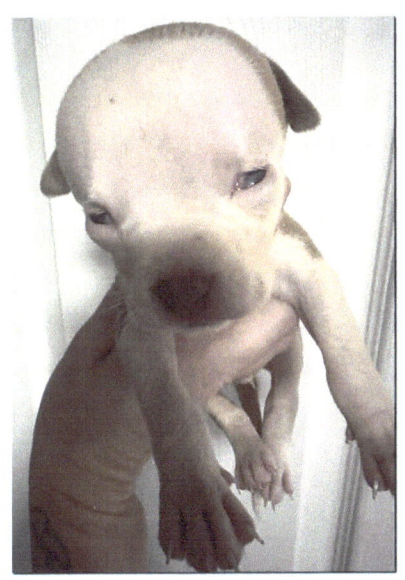

Isaiah, above, when he was first rescued. He was so tiny! Below, Isaiah, today, at five months old.

Isaiah is one of the lucky puppies saved by Blazin' Trails Bottle Babies. He has been on daily medication, but at five months old, he is now big enough (at long last) to safely undergo life-saving surgery. The operation will cost his small rescue $15,000, but Isaiah's life matters and he has the chance at a long, pain-free future with a loving forever family once he has recovered.

Isaiah is so adorable and deserving of all the good things life has to offer. We are rooting for this precious little fellow to heal and thrive!

Meet Benjamin

Benjamin was abandoned at two weeks old in the parking lot of a veterinary office, his skin severely urine scalded. He must have been in horrific pain.

Thank goodness he came into the care of Blazin' Trails Bottle Babies. The rescue treated his terrible burns and resulting infection and set tiny Benjamin on the path to well-being and the carefree life every puppy deserves.

Fast forward to today. Benjamin is now a young adult at one year old. He has been adopted into a loving forever home with a doggie sibling and human mom he cherishes.

Benjamin's journey has taken him from a life of agony to one free from pain and full of love. What a happy ending for this handsome sweetheart!

From helpless to happy, Benjamin is one of the lucky ones whose life has been transformed. He no longer hurts. He is safe; healthy; and as is evident in the photos below, living a life of ease.

Meet Blaze ♥

Blaze was the tiny one who started it all for Blazin' Trails Bottle Babies. In fact, he is the group's namesake!

Blaze came to the rescue at a mere 24 hours old. His mother had chewed off one of his front paws, a tragedy which apparently can happen in cases where the adult dog is not suited to motherhood.

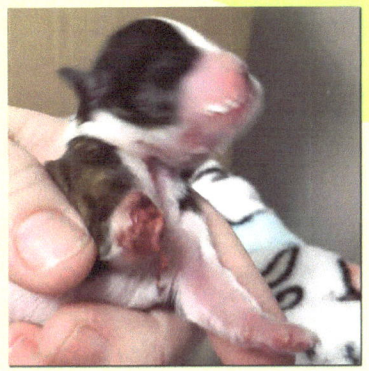

Blaze, above, just one day old.

Through caring for Blaze, the rescue quickly discovered how few resources and veterinary care exist for neonates (dogs under four weeks old), so the group had to learn and navigate how best to help him on its own.

The research Blazin' Trails undertook is now established as the rescue's protocols for best practices in neonate puppy care.

Above, a happy "tri-pawed" pup. Below, Blaze, today.

In its infancy, Blazin' Trails anticipated helping just a few rescues each year. However, last year the group rescued nearly 200 orphaned newborn puppies!

And what of Blaze today?

Well, he has been home with the rescue's founder since Day 1 and now confidently shows the "newbies" who come through the door how things are done!

Meet Zero ♥

Zero was dumped in a field along with 16 other newborn puppies. She was discovered when a lawnmower ran over her tiny body, causing a severe laceration to her neck.

Unfortunately, attempts by the vet to suture the large area were unsuccessful, leaving this poor baby with a gaping wound only meticulous care and time proved able to heal.

Despite such an agonizing and challenging start in life, Zero is now a happy and healthy girl. She is six months young and has been welcomed into a loving forever home.

If not for the diligent and sustained care Zero was blessed to receive from Blazin' Trails Bottle Babies, this precious puppy would have stood no chance at survival. Instead, we are thrilled to know that, today, Zero has zero chance of anything but a bright and love-filled future ahead!

From the top, Zero's initial, devastating injury, followed by an image of her gradually healing wound. Despite an enormous and incredibly painful injury, Zero was nonetheless a sweetheart and (dare we say?!) a bit of a party girl, as evidenced by her "dress-up" photo. Above left, Zero, fully recovered and the image of the darling she has always been.

Meet Tyson ❤

Tyson's story is, in part, a mystery. He had already been rescued and was in a shelter's care but, somehow, at just four weeks of age, was horribly burned along the length of his back. No determination has been made as to how this occurred.

Nevertheless, at that point, given his neonate status, his medical condition was dire, so Blazin' Trails Bottle Babies stepped up to take tiny Tyson into its fold. It is heartbreaking to fathom the pain he must have endured.

Through the long process of caring for Tyson's terrible burn wounds, his foster mom fell in love with this brave and precious darling and decided she couldn't let him go.

One look at those soulful eyes and hilarious giant ears, and it's easy to see why!

Way to win everyone over, Tyson! Now eight months old, this cutie is still a baby but growing, healthy, and living a most happy life!

From top to bottom, baby Tyson's burns, when fresh and still healing, and Tyson, happy warrior.

Our Work and Our Little Wonders in Pictures

About the Rescue

If it hadn't been for the pandemic, Cats of Davidson might never have gotten started. Working from home, founder Roni LaBarbera became aware of the large feral cat population in the town of Davidson. She borrowed equipment from a friend and taught herself how to trap, so the cats could be transported to clinics to be spayed/neutered and vaccinated.

Along the way, she realized that many of these feral cats were producing kittens at an alarming rate, and that is when she teamed up with another Davidson resident, Amy Doughten, to create a plan to foster and adopt the kittens.

In the ensuing years, Cats of Davidson has spayed/neutered numerous feral cats and adopted out hundreds of kittens. What began as 2 friends trying to make a difference in the community has evolved into a nonprofit organization with 501(c)(3) status and a 5-member board.

Cats of Davidson currently feeds and cares for five feral cat communities in the town of Davidson, supplying food, veterinary care as needed, and preventative medications. The work of the rescue is wholly supported by donations, grants, and volunteers.

How to Contact and How to Help

As a charitable organization, Cats of Davidson is entirely supported by the generosity of the community and so grateful for its ongoing support.
The rescue is composed of devoted, home-based volunteers who trap feral cats; coordinate their sterilization, recovery, and subsequent release; participate in community events; and manage the kitten adoption program.

The rescue's web site: http://www.catsofdavidson.org

To view adoptable kittens, visit:

Web Site: https://catsofdavidson.org/adoption/

Adopt a Pet: https://www.adoptapet.com/shelter/
184872-cats-of-davidson-davidson-north-carolina

Donations are always welcome and appreciated. Contributions may be made in any of the following ways:

Amazon Wish List: https://www.amazon.com/hz/wishlist/ls/
7329N60GL0YD?ref_=wl_share

Venmo: @CatsofDavidsonNC

Zeffy: https://www.zeffy.com/en-US/donation-form/
purr-sistent-giving-support-kittens-and-cats-every-month

Meet Hershey ♥

Hershey's story began on a quiet front porch where a kind couple had built a cozy shelter for a feral mama cat named Candy and her three newborn kittens. Tucked safely away from the weather, the little family should have been off to a straightforward start. But it soon became clear all was not well.

Two of the kittens appeared in need of medical attention, and the couple did not know where to turn. Luckily, that's when Cats of Davidson stepped in.

Right away, the team noticed something unusual about the tiniest tabby. His face looked smooshed, and his body was much smaller than that of his siblings. Simply put, he didn't match the rest of his family.

Above, Hershey was a tiny baby, underweight relative to his age and failing to grow despite nursing and receiving high-quality kitten food.

The team even wondered, initially, if Candy might have "kitten-napped" him (rescued him elsewhere and claimed him as her own).

The baby was named Hershey, and though he was as sweet as his name, he worried everyone. As days passed, the other surviving kitten grew strong and round, but Hershey didn't. His foster weighed him carefully each day, hoping to see his numbers climb. However, although he was still nursing and his foster was offering high-calorie kitten food, his appetite was low and the scale barely moved. The rescue feared Hershey's story might end far too soon.

But then came a moment of hope. A thoughtful veterinarian took a closer look and wondered if the problem might be hidden on the inside. Tests were run, and the answer was finally discovered: Hershey had been born without a thyroid gland.

The thyroid controls the speed of the body's metabolism, and Hershey's tiny body was missing this essential ability!

Thanks to medication and close monitoring, Hershey slowly began to change. His appetite appeared. Then his energy. And finally, his growth. Week by week, the once fragile kitten became sturdier, brighter, and more playful. His foster loved him deeply, cheering every ounce gained and every milestone achieved.

Above and to the left, Hershey, all grown up. He has gone from being the cutest tiny baby into an adorable adult. It's safe to say we would all love to give Hershey a kiss!

Then Hershey's forever family found him! They saw him not as a sick kitten, but as a brave one with a gentle soul and a powerful will to live. Hershey went home, grew into the big and happy cat he is today, and left his rough beginning behind. Now there are no more worries—only purrs, joy, and the blessing of a cherished pet given the chance to thrive.

Meet Simon

Simon's story begins with a lucky break. A driver spotted the tiny kitten lying near a road, starving and barely moving. His mother and siblings had moved on. His belly was round and swollen with worms, and his legs did not work as they should. He was cold, frightened, and far too small to be alone. The good Samaritan took him to Cats of Davidson, where he was wrapped in warmth, given a name (Simon), and promised he would never be alone again.

With gentle hands and patient hearts, the rescue treated his sick belly, fed him carefully, and ensured he rested. Day by day, Simon grew stronger. He learned to hold himself up and, eventually, to take trembling steps. As Simon recovered, however, it became clear his movements remained shaky and his balance unsteady.

Above, Simon was an adorable but messy eater at first. With cerebellar hypoplasia, a kitten must try really hard to focus on what it's trying to do. That tends to make its head and even its body tremble (hence, a bit of a mess, though they are so worth it). As a CH kitty matures, it typically finds ways to compensate, at least somewhat, for challenging activities.

Simon had cerebellar hypoplasia (CH), known informally as wobbly cat syndrome. CH is a neurological condition in which the portion of the brain responsible for balance and coordination (the cerebellum) doesn't fully form while a kitten is developing in the womb. CH is not painful, and it doesn't worsen over time. Neither is it contagious. It is discovered as a kitten begins to walk upright and its unsteadiness does not diminish over the ensuing weeks. Depending on the level of impairment, CH can make walking, jumping, or even standing and eating somewhat tricky. Most CH cats fall into the mild category and just experience the world with a bit more wobble than most.

Simon didn't mind, as he didn't know he was different. With love and patience, he learned important skills. He was gently trained to potty at regular times and held safely in the litter box until his body adapted. Over time, Simon surprised his caretakers by using the box entirely on his own. He also made friends with the resident cats, wobbling up to them with a hopeful flick of his tail. And one day, much to everybody's amazement, he figured out the stairs, one careful but determined step at a time.

Above, Simon, napping worry free.

Yet even with all that progress, his humans worried. Disabled kittens are often overlooked. Would anyone see Simon for who he truly was? The answer, it would turn out, was a resounding yes. The perfect application arrived!

A man who uses a wheelchair, his wife, and their two children wished to adopt a cat with special needs. They understood that bodies come in many forms, all worthy of love. And when they met Simon, it was instantly clear: this was his family! Today, Simon thrives in his forever home. He proves every day that being different doesn't mean being less. It's just about finding the place—and the people—where you belong.

Meet Duffman ♥

If these true stories had traditional titles, this one would have to be "Duffman's Smart Choice."

Once upon a time, there was an orange-and-white cat named Duffman, who lived outside. Life on his own wasn't easy. His fur was dirty, he smelled a bit stinky, and his tummy was often empty. Still, Duffman was friendly at heart and believed that kindness could be found—even in unexpected places.

One day, a Cats of Davidson trapper was out trying to help a mama cat. She set out some tasty treats, hoping the mama would come by. Instead, a different cat appeared. It was Duffman.

Above , Duffman had infected bite wounds from a coyote or large dog when he first approached a Cats of Davidson volunteer for help.

He trotted right up, sniffed the air, and decided those treats smelled way too good to ignore. But instead of grabbing a snack and running away, Duffman did something surprising. He walked right up to the trapper, began to purr, and rubbed against her legs as if to say, "Hello. I think I need help."

The trapper noticed right away that something was wrong. Duffman had dried blood and large bite marks along his neck and shoulders. He had clearly been attacked and injured severely and was fortunate to be alive.

She checked him for a microchip. None. He wasn't neutered either. Wanting to help, she opened a cat carrier, tossed in a few treats, and held her breath. Duffman didn't hesitate. He walked right in and laid down. He didn't cry. He didn't fuss. It was as if he knew this was his chance, and Duffman made a very smart choice!

At the veterinarian's office, the news was serious. His wounds were infected, likely from a coyote or large dog, and without help he might not have survived. Thanks to quick action, he received medicine, antibiotics, and lots of care in a medical foster home, where he could rest and heal.

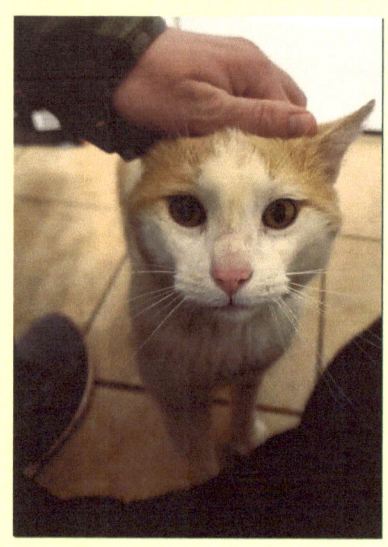

Above , Duffman was a love from the moment he approached his rescuer. Below, Duffman, now a spoiled indoor kitty, as every cat should be.

Once he'd recovered, Cats of Davidson knew Duffman couldn't go back to the place where he'd been hurt. He was far too sweet, and far too hungry for love, to be on his own again. And then came the happiest chapter in Duffman's story. He was adopted by a wonderful family with a big catio, where he could safely enjoy fresh air and sunshine. And because every hero should have a sidekick, the family also adopted a kitten who looked just like him to be his new best friend.

Duffman had trusted the right person at the right moment, and it saved his life! Now, his days are filled with naps, purrs, and the joy of knowing he is finally home.

About the Rescue

Founded in 2019, Killer Kitties Rescue 2.0 is a 501(c)(3) nonprofit organization and the sole cat-only rescue operating in Stanly County, North Carolina.

The volunteer-only group's primary mission is to save cats and kittens from shelters with traditionally high rates of euthanasia and find them loving forever homes. The rescue also promotes the spaying, neutering, and vaccination of pets by connecting owners with resources in surrounding communities offering low-cost veterinary services.

How to Contact and How to Help

Reach out with questions by e-mail, and follow Killer Kitties Rescue 2.0 on social media to keep up with its latest news.

E-mail: killerkittiesrescue@yahoo.com

Facebook: https://www.facebook.com/profile.php?id= 100064863365537

Instagram: @killer_kitties_rescue

How to Contact and How to Help, Continued

To meet the rescue's adoptable cats and kittens, please visit:

Adopt a Pet: https://www.adoptapet.com/shelter/158259-killer-kitties-rescue-oakboro-north-carolina

Petfinder: https://www.petfinder.com/member/us/nc/oakboro/killer-kitties-rescue-nc1078/

Donations are always needed and gratefully accepted through one of the following portals:

Cash App: $killerkitties19

CUDDLY: https://cuddly.com/partner/59953?srsltid=AfmBOor6WTDViL4AlS5wTzE29uYd0bU7imtIXTL5cDSKTWpxVXCrph6y

PayPal: killerkittiesrescue@yahoo.com

Venmo: @killerkitties19 (last four digits: 0014)

Meet Rajah

Returns are a sad fact of animal adoption not often discussed. Most, if not all, rescues agree to take back the pets they adopt should things not work out in the near or long term. Why? Well, it is very personal to these small groups. The rescues do not want the beloved creatures they healed and fostered, sometimes for months or even years, to end up turned in at an animal shelter.

Returns may occur quickly and for a variety of reasons. Other times they happen many years later. Adopters may become seriously ill, disabled, or pass away. Or as was the case with Rajah, unforeseen allergies may be the culprit.

Above and below, for Rajah, his removal from the home and people he loved was a very stressful and depressing event. Pets often suffer greatly in such situations, being thrust into a whole new place without knowing why. It is a painful thing for all involved to witness their grief and distress.

Rajah was adopted as a kitten from Killer Kitties Rescue 2.0 and was a well-loved and well-cared-for pet for nearly 6 years. His adopter then married and had a baby Rajah adored. Rajah even liked to sleep with the little one.

However, the baby proved to be highly allergic to cats, to the point of respiratory distress. Rajah's continued presence in the home was not possible. Even with cat food now on the market that can substantially reduce the amount of allergens a cat produces, it is not a guaranteed or overnight solution and time could not be spared. Sadly, Rajah had to be returned.

Rajah remained in the care of Killer Kitties for nearly a year. The rescue posted him for re-adoption regularly, but it is a challenge to find an adopter for a middle-aged cat. One potential adopter did apply, only to later object to the rescue group's thorough application process and change his mind.

Very recently, however, the rescue was able to place Rajah in the "Kitten Klubhouse" (an indoor visitation room) of a local business called wicks & whiskers in Charlotte (www.wicksandwhiskers.com).

Above, the handsome and majestic Rajah. To the left, Rajah, displaying his spunk with a toy at the wicks & whiskers store in Charlotte. Through that innovative experiment, Rajah was successful in winning over his new family!

The shop offers a "kitten and kandle experience," through which customers are able to create custom-designed and -scented candles and meet cats and kittens available for adoption. The store has made a mutually beneficial arrangement with Killer Kitties Rescue 2.0, and in just 6 months the rescue has been able to find loving forever homes for 40 kitties through this venue, including a new home for Rajah! The rescue is overjoyed for Rajah and grateful to wicks & whiskers and his new family for this wonderful boy's second chance at a happy life as a beloved pet!

Meet Johnny Depp ♥

Johnny Depp was found by one of Killer Kitties' fosters, who happened to be out trying to catch other homeless cats for spaying and neutering. He was only a few weeks old and had severely infected eyes.

He was named by the rescue's adoption coordinator, who thought him a handsome little fellow despite the terrible condition of his eyes.

Johnny Depp spent the next several months on antibiotics, as the rescue worked valiantly to save his vision. Through the process, everyone fell in love with his sweet personality and his patient acceptance of myriad treatments.

Ultimately, only one of his eyes proved "save-able," but it was a huge victory nevertheless, as it meant Johnny Depp would retain at least partial vision.

He underwent enucleation of his right eye once he was big enough to safely face anesthesia and surgery, and then he had another period of recovery before he could be ready for adoption.

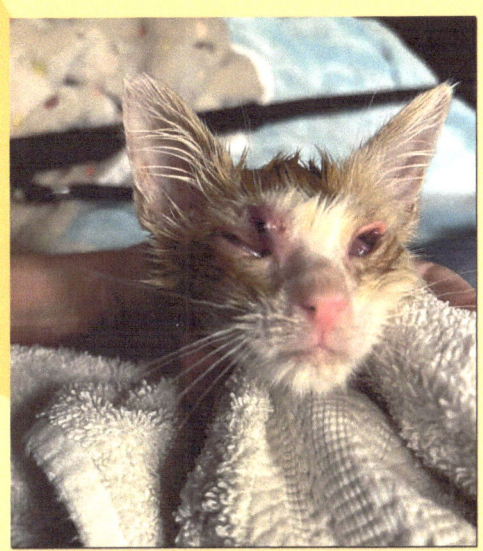

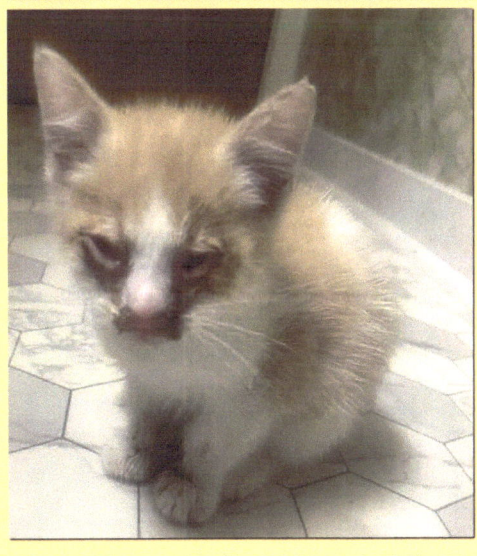

Above, the rescue wasn't sure, at first, if Johnny Depp's eyesight could be saved, but it was determined to try.

Lucky for Johnny Depp, one of Killer Kitties' past adopters fell in love with him.

Repeat adopters, with a proven track record as loving pet parents, make a rescue's decision an easy one—though maybe not so easy for his foster mom, who had fallen in love with this sweet boy while caring for him all those months.

Today, Johnny Depp is nearly two years young and adored in his forever home! He has a human sister who loves him and two kitty siblings with whom he has built a close relationship.

Movie star or not, these days life is "looking" good for Johnny Depp!

Above, Johnny Depp, now fully recovered and quite the handsome kitty. To the right, Johnny Depp in the arms of his loving human sister.

Our Purpose and Our Pride and Joy

Our Purpose and Our Pride and Joy, Continued

About the Rescue

Miles to Go is a 501(c)(3) nonprofit organization that has dedicated the last 6 years to saving neonatal orphan kittens who require intensive care—kittens who are likely to be euthanized at many shelters and whose care is beyond the scope of many fosters. Miles to Go is committed to providing a safe, loving environment and the socialization required for kittens to grow and thrive.

Miles to Go believes every vulnerable life deserves love, access to medical expertise, and compassionate care for the mind, body, and spirit. The rescue strives to raise awareness of the unique needs of kittens under four weeks through community outreach programs, via collaboration with medical experts, and by supporting other fosters and caregivers.

The rescue also works to raise awareness of important milestones and issues that impact neonatal kittens specifically—and to educate people about their care and promote a network of support for the kittens and their future forever families.

How to Contact and How to Help, Continued

Keep up with Miles to Go and its precious babies on social media:

Facebook: https://www.facebook.com/MilesToGoKittenRehab/

Instagram: @milestogokittenrehab

Web Site: milestogokittenrehab.com

View the rescue's adoptable kittens on Petfinder:

https://www.petfinder.com/member/us/nc/currie/miles-to-go-kitten-rehab-nc1305/

Support Miles to Go's mission in any of the following ways:

Amazon Wish List: https://amzn.to/3P3ajCM

Cash App: $jwitkowski

PayPal: milestogokittenrehab@gmail.com
https://www.paypal.com/us/fundraiser/charity/5394395

Venmo: MilestoGoKittenRehab (last four digits: 9458)
https://venmo.com/u/MilestoGoKittenRehab

Meet Howie

Howie's story began a few weeks before he came to Miles to Go Kitten Rehab. He was part of a litter of three babies the rescue was expecting to receive, though at first it only received Howie's sister. At the time, Miles to Go was given the explanation that the other two tinies had gone to an alternate rehabber.

Confused as to why the litter was divided, Miles to Go followed up with an offer to take all the babies. It was at that point the rescue learned the other two siblings had actually gone to "someone's mom" rather than a rescue experienced in caring for neonates (kittens less than four weeks old).

Concerned, Miles to Go persisted in attempting to help, offering any and all support it could. Its offers were rebuffed.

Above, at three weeks old, Howie should have been growing plump and thriving like his sister, who had been in the rescue's care for two weeks.

Two long weeks later, the individual with the neonate brothers contacted Miles to Go to say one of the babies was dying. It was then that Howie and his brother were finally taken into the rescue's fold. Tragically, Howie's brother was skeletally thin and never even got a name before passing away a few hours later. The rescue was, at once, both livid and devastated about his suffering and needless death. Howie, the remaining brother, was in extremely poor condition as well.

Howie was "smothered in fleas," the worst infestation, in fact, the rescue had ever seen. Howie was also a bit "off," as if the proverbial lights were on but no one was home.

His eyes bulged and only somewhat focused ... some of the time. If Howie's tiny body were tilted in in one direction and then back again in the opposite direction, one of his eyes

Above, Howie exhibited odd characteristics when first rescued. He was the cutest little thing, but there was uncertainty about what was wrong and whether the little guy would pull through.

would remain "stuck" for several moments before adjusting to the positional change. Additionally, his pupils moved at two different speeds.

Working with the rescue's vet, possible medical explanations were debated and eliminated. Was Howie blind? No. Was he deaf? No. Was Howie's strange detachment the result of starvation, flea anemia, or brain damage? Both the rescue and vet were unsure and uncertain about his viability, but Miles to Go was committed to doing the best it could by Howie nonetheless. So the rescue took Howie home to do the one thing he did with exceptional gusto: eat!

At first, Howie was only vaguely interested in humans, but he was head over heels in love with wet food (though he had no idea how to eat it)! He turned every meal into a joyous, full body bath experience. Raised bowls meant nothing, as food was meant to be slathered on. Slowly, Howie became more aware of his sister as they shared meals. He began to change, making eye contact for the first time with the rescue's founder. Then he found his purr, and he discovered that full body dance snuggles are one of life's greatest joys.

Despite everything he'd been through, he became the pure embodiment of love in a small soul. He became a kitten who was happy to be alive and enjoying every moment of his life!

Howie and his sister graduated as valedictorians of Miles to Go's "Good Citizen Academy." They traveled with the rescue's founder to public festivals, craft fairs, and comic conventions.

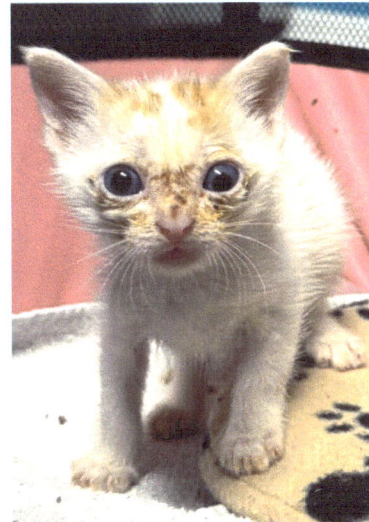
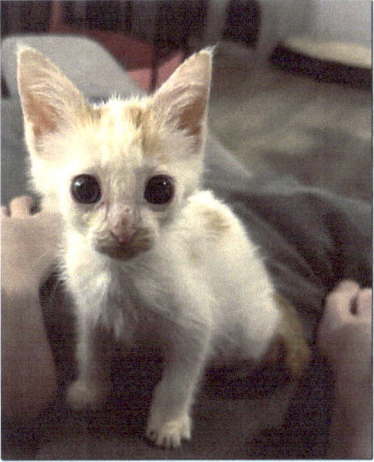

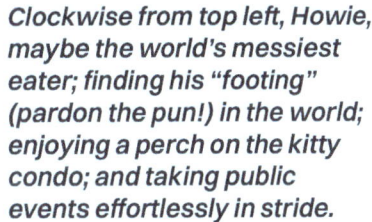

Clockwise from top left, Howie, maybe the world's messiest eater; finding his "footing" (pardon the pun!) in the world; enjoying a perch on the kitty condo; and taking public events effortlessly in stride.

Eventually both Howie and his sister were reserved for adoption. However, in the week before their placement, the rescue's founder took note of Howie's growing obsession with her dog. While all the babies invariably show some level of interest in Draper the dog, Howie was constantly following, cuddling with, and clinging to him.

She asked the two adoptive families if they would be willing to switch kittens, as one of the families has a pup and the founder believed "in her gut" that Howie needed a doggie friend. Thankfully, the adopters graciously agreed, and it proved to be the right call.

Howie now lives his absolute best life with his dog brother, safe and happy and adored. Today, Howie is exactly where he was always meant to be!

Above, Howie, thriving in the perfect forever home with his very best friend, the family dog. Their bonded relationship is a testament to the fact that true love is truly blind.

SAVE THE CLEFTS

RESCUE

About the Rescue

Save The Clefts Rescue (STCR) was founded out of a desire to save special needs animals that are often euthanized at birth. The founder had been independently saving pups for years but realized she needed help to advocate for, educate about, and assume financial responsibility for these precious animals on a larger scale. She formed the 501(c)(3) nonprofit rescue in 2018 to formalize those efforts.

Founded and still operating in North Carolina, the rescue now has a network of fosters in Georgia, Missouri, Ohio, Pennsylvania, South Carolina, and Virginia, with volunteers in many other states helping to get these amazing babies to trained fosters quickly.

The biggest hurdle faced by a cleft palate and lip puppy, due to the deformity, is its inability to suckle at birth. Therefore, each call about a puppy is an emergency, as newborns must be fed as soon as possible after birth. STCR volunteers drop everything to pick up and deliver puppies to their fosters, to ensure the greatest chance of survival. Neonates are tube fed around the clock every two to three hours until old enough to be weaned onto kibble.

About the Rescue, Continued

STCR is blessed with volunteer pilots, ground transport, around-the-clock caregivers and event/fundraising volunteers. It has created and maintains a nationwide database of rescues and volunteers that come together for special needs animals to save thousands of lives each year.

To date, no corrective surgery has been needed on any of the pups saved by STCR, and the rescue has played a pivotal role in a study conducted at the North Carolina State Veterinary Hospital, whose goal was to determine whether costly surgery is, in fact, always needed to save these animals' lives and give them a good quality of life. The study found this NOT to be the case, leading to changes in medical care across the veterinary community.

Since its formation, STCR has saved hundreds of puppies and four kittens, all of whom have gone on to enjoy happy and healthy lives. And recently, fulfilling a goal to become more active in the human cleft community, STCR shared its pups at a University of North Carolina Craniofacial Center event, where cleft-affected humans and animals met and bonded. It was pure joy! In fact, STCR has adopted seven puppies to families with cleft-affected children, with incredible impacts on the lives of everyone involved.

How to Contact and How to Help

Follow along with STCR on Facebook, TikTok, and Instagram @savetheclefts. If help with a cleft puppy is needed, or to volunteer, adopt, or support its cause, please visit the rescue's above social media sites or its web site at www.savetheclefts.org.

Meet Tennison Mars

Tennison Mars, known as Tenny, came to the rescue at just twelve hours old. His breeder, loving and attentive, noticed immediately that two of his newborn puppies had cleft lips and palates and would need specialized care to pull through. He reached out to Save The Clefts, experts in saving cleft-affected neonates.

Without intervention, Tenny wouldn't have survived. He was dependent on round-the-clock care, hand reared, and tube fed. With dedicated neonatal care, Tenny grew stronger, steadier, and more confident.

While Tenny will live with this condition for the rest of his life, it does not define his limits. He is full of joy, nurturing, thoughtful, smart, lovingly childlike, and wonderfully naïve. He moves through the world with quiet intention, as if every step matters. He still suckles his blankets, a tender reminder of how his life began and how deeply he seeks comfort and connection.

Above, Tenny, being tube fed. At left, his cleft lip and palate meant he could not latch and suckle.

Below, Tenny, today, adorable veteran traveler.

He loves his forever person beyond measure: his foster mom. He didn't have far to go to find her. He also loves balls. (In that order, his mom says, though sometimes it's a close call.) He is extraordinary with other dogs, serving as a remarkable foster brother to countless puppies, many born with the same condition. In short, Tenny is proof that limits are often imagined rather than inherited ... and that love *can* conquer all.

Meet Swagger ♥

Swagger James Mars ("Swagger," for short) was not cleft affected but was a unique kind of fragile, and his breeder wanted him to have the rescue's special kind of love and resources to ensure he had the best life ever. He came to Save the Clefts at eight weeks old, a wee bit of a baby at just five pounds.

While he was never a failure in the rescue's eyes, Swagger was categorized as such by veterinarians. He was born with juvenile kidney disease, brachycephalic obstructive airway syndrome (BOAS), seizures, and musculoskeletal development issues with his legs.

To the rescue, Swagger was not a "special needs" puppy, but a special miracle, with a personality that lights up any room he enters. He's been living on love since the day he came to Save the Clefts!

Swagger doesn't know about any of this and doesn't let anything stop him from enjoying life to the fullest. He recently

Above, there was nothing cuter than Swagger as a baby! And below, as an adult, one could easily insist there's still nothing cuter than Swagger!

celebrated his third birthday and lives with his devoted family in the mountains, where he enjoys hiking; canoeing; riding in the family's off-road vehicle; and most fun of all, splashing in his pool.

We don't know Swagger's future, but we do know it will always be full of love!

Clockwise from above left, Swagger, doing a bit of skinny dipping; ready for adventure, with his seatbelt on, of course, like any responsible off roader; and dressed up for his birthday festivities!

Meet Beau ❤

Beau was born with what his foster family called the "Grand Canyon" of clefts: hard and soft pallet. Along with that came kidney disease. The family agreed to be long-term hospice fosters to Beau through Save the Clefts. The family's goal was to give Beau the most loving, normal, happy, and healthy life they could until his body couldn't carry on any longer; and they did just that.

Beau loved his pack, both his canine siblings and his humans. He was adored by his Mamaw and Grandaddy Jack beyond words. They would cover their couch upon the family's arrival for a visit, so the dogs would be as much at home as the people. Beau's human siblings, Cole, Abby, and Lilly, loved him deeply. In fact, all who knew Beau, and what the family was doing for him, prayed and rooted for him with every bit of energy they had.

Above, Beau, as a baby.

Beau loved to run free in the mountains and play in the creek with his sister, BB, but he most loved riding in the "side by side" and being in New River with the best dog dad ever, Bill. He also loved traveling in the car, so the family indulged him with numerous car rides. He loved to snuggle, too, as well as have his own space at times. And toys? Beau loved them all!

Below left, Beau, wading in the creek. Below right, Beau, surrounded by his beloved doggie pack.

Beau has gone on his eternal journey now, leaving this world in his foster mother's arms but held in the hearts of the family that loved him forever.

In the words of his foster mom, "If you have the chance to have a Beau, do it!" You will be rewarded beyond measure.

Above, Beau, sleeping peacefully. Despite his medical challenges, we should all be so fortunate as this precious boy was to have lived a life overflowing with joy and love.

Meet Gia Grace

Gia Grace came to Save the Clefts all the way from Alabama. She had been thrown from a vehicle, was saved by horrified witnesses, and was taken to a rescue. That rescue contacted Save the Clefts upon discovering a cleft lip with minor palate involvement, to ensure Gia Grace received the proper care.

From there, Gia Grace made her way to her forever home with her human mom, a then-17-year-old young lady who, herself, was cleft affected. In fact, Gia Grace and her mom have matching cleft lips on the same side and were Save the Clefts Rescue's first pairing of a cleft human and dog!

Despite being cleft affected, today Gia behaves like any "normal" dog. She is a lover and incredibly smart, confident, sassy, silly, and full of life. She adores everyone she meets and enjoys going on walks, giving kisses, playing with her cockapoo best friend, and lying in the sunshine. She even tries to enjoy car rides. Her favorite thing of all, though, is snuggling with her cleft-affected mom whenever she can.

Gia Grace is a testament to the connection between humans and animals with cleft conditions. Her loving presence has increased her mom's confidence and passion for expanding public awareness about cleft conditions in humans and animals alike.

Above, Gia Grace was one darling baby! Below, with her favorite person in the world, her likewise cleft-affected mom! What a perfect pair they are!

Meet Ridiculous

Ridiculous, known as "Ridic," is one of those dogs whose name tells you everything you need to know. He is sweet, goofy, and truly a joy to be around.

Ridic was accidentally stomped by his mother when he was only a few days old. That single accident caused mobility, nerve, vision, and cognitive damage.

Ridic has been blessed with a volunteer physical therapist and chiropractor, and those two men gave the gift of their time for months to ensure Ridic could walk. Ridic is able to see, though not normally, and he can understand, just in a different way.

He often turns his head sideways to focus—and when he is spoken to, it is clear he understands every word, but in a wonderfully childlike way. And if he doesn't like what is being said, he can be adorably defiant about it!

Ridic has been diagnosed with scoliosis (a sideways curvature of the spine, causing it to appear in a "C" or "S" shape) and kyphosis (a severe outward curvature of the upper spine, resulting in a hunched appearance of the upper back), caused by nerve damage and compensation.

Above, Ridic, resting after physical therapy. Below, Ridic, with his adorably cocked head.

Ridic's family says he may be the smartest dog they've ever had, with the largest vocabulary of any of them to date. He is proof that being different does not mean being less. His family would love to save more dogs just like Ridic in the future.

Clockwise from the top right, Ridic, with his dear friend, Javin, from Sterner Physical Therapy. Javin volunteered many hours, over months, to design and implement Ridic's physical therapy. Ridic still sees Javin, to this day, for periodic evaluations. It is clear to see the love they have for one another.

ANIMAL RESCUE

About the Rescue

Simply put, Sunkissed Acres NC strives to help as many animals and people as it can, with the dream of one day having no animals needing to be saved. This may be a lofty vision, but it is one the organization is working its hardest every day to realize.

In 2024 and 2025 alone, Sunkissed Acres NC trapped, spayed or neutered, and vaccinated nearly 900 "community"/feral cats and kittens, which means those unfortunate souls will no longer be able to produce offspring to further increase the number of homeless cats in the Charlotte metropolitan area. Plus, they will be far less likely to engage in the territorial fighting that leads to life-altering injuries; far less likely to contract and spread a variety of life-threatening illnesses, thus giving them healthier, more dignified lives; and far more likely to possibly be socialized and adopted as pets in the future.

Over those same 2 years, Sunkissed Acres NC has also helped more than 150 cats and dogs stay in their homes by financially supporting the essential veterinary care and medications their guardians were otherwise unable to afford. That care has included spaying/neutering, vaccinating, and microchipping residents' pets; donating treatments for fleas and fungal infections; and covering the cost of surgery and other

About the Rescue, Continued

acute care for a wide range of medically compromising conditions. In the aftermath of Hurricane Helene in late 2024, Sunkissed Acres NC delivered over 10 van loads of food and related pet supplies to the devastated citizens of the Asheville, North Carolina, area. The rescue's efforts to assist in all of these regards have meant the difference between pets being able to stay with their owners or being relinquished to face, at best, a terrifying change in circumstances or, at worst, euthanasia.

Through 2024 and 2025, Sunkissed Acres NC has also successfully socialized and adopted over 400 cats and dogs into loving forever homes, thoroughly screening potential adopters to ensure each animal is placed into a welcoming, safe, and financially viable environment where it will be loved as an integral family member and never again go hungry or suffer without medical care.

How to Contact and How to Help

For adoption information or to foster, please visit the rescue on Facebook (facebook.com/sunkissedacresnc) or the web (sunkissedacresnc.org). Donations are always needed and welcome. Your tax-deductible gift may be made in any of the following ways:

Cash App: $kitty24680
PayPal: sunkissedacreskitties@hotmail.com
Venmo: @sunkissedacreskitties
Zelle: sunkissedacreskitties@hotmail.com (704-451-9974)

Meet Levi

Petite Levi, still a kitten at the time, showed up at a mechanic's shop with a very obviously broken leg (the bone was visible in two areas). He was fed bits of dry food tossed on the ground and allowed to remain in that condition for over a month. His pain must have been unimaginable.

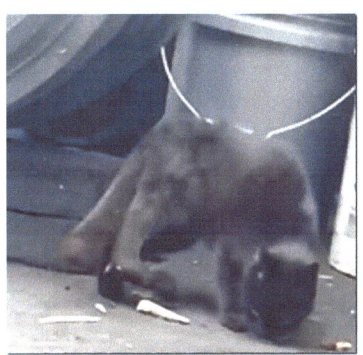

A concerned person finally reached out to an area trapper, who rescued him the same day. He was to be fostered by a lady who had just lost her beloved senior amputee two days before, but she knew she could not afford a costly surgery at the time. Sunkissed Acres NC ran a fundraiser for Levi, and the community stepped up to help this baby, raising everything needed. He was able to undergo surgery the very same weekend he was saved.

Levi, whose name is now Scout, has since been adopted by an amazing family. He has two cat siblings and humans who adore him. They say he is even "trained" to watch football on the TV with his human dad. And three legs do not slow him down!

Above, Levi searching for food with a broken leg. Also above, after rescue. Below, Levi (now Scout) has a home!

When he was rescued at just eight months old, Levi weighed what a kitten half his age should (only four pounds). He has remained a smaller cat, but he has had a giant-sized impact on his foster, the community (he's a local celebrity these days), and the family he can now proudly call his own!

Meet Buster ❤

Buster was quite the ladies' man in his pre-neuter days. It took the founder of Sunkissed Acres NC six months to catch him. At the time, Buster was estimated to be 11 years old, so he had years of history that will never be fully known.

At his first vet visit, Buster tested positive for feline immunodeficiency virus (FIV), sometimes called feline "AIDS." It simply meant his immune system was not as effective as that of a normal cat. FIV is transmitted through deep blood-to-blood transfer, such as through bad cat fights between unaltered males vying for territory.

The good news about FIV is that it is not easily spread. FIV-positive cats can live with FIV-negative cats. They can share food and water dishes; groom one another; and play with, wrestle with, and even nibble on each other, all without issue. Most importantly, once they are safe indoors, FIV-positive cats have a normal life expectancy. Buster was certainly a shining example of that fact, living for nearly 24 years!

Buster was adored by his human mom, everyone he met, and by the hundreds of rescued cats and kittens he nurtured. He was everyone's favorite grandpa and a true poster child (or old man, in his case) for the rewards of loving an FIV-positive cat.

Buster, among the most loving cats one could ever hope to know. He is still mourned years later.

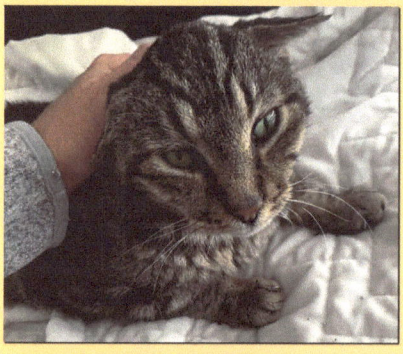

Meet Baby B. ❤

Baby B. came to Sunkissed Acres at five weeks old. The rescue had been searching for her mom for three weeks, knowing she was still pregnant or had recently given birth. The rescue trapped 23 other young mothers and kittens at the wooded site, spaying, vaccinating, and returning the feral moms (a process called trap-neuter-release, or TNR) and finding homes for all the babies.

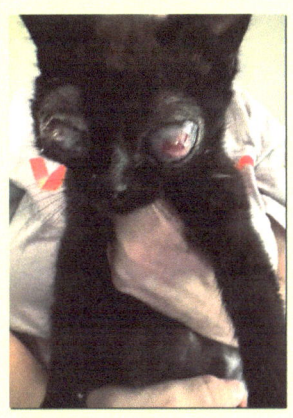

Baby B. was found inside a broken-down truck in the hottest part of summer. Her trapper reached out to multiple rescues about her case, all of which advised euthanasia due to the terrible condition of her eyes. But Sunkissed Acres stepped up to help. Baby B. was rushed to the vet, who took her home and treated her for three weeks before returning her to the rescue's care to continue her medical journey. Baby B. was syringe fed to help her grow enough for surgery to remove her irreparably damaged eyes. At four months, she was finally able to undergo enucleation of both.

Above, Baby B., as she appeared when saved. Below, Baby B., after surgery and on her way to the perfect home.

Baby B. has stolen the hearts of everyone she's met. You'd never know this little one is blind or faced even a single day in misery. She is living proof that miracles happen. She has boundless gratitude and love to give and reminds us all to live with joy. And as for her own joyful ending? Well, Baby B. is now the precious pet of the very vet who saved (and named) her! The "B" stands for Bright Eyes, which is exactly what she is, with or without sight!

Meet Sammie

Sammie is a beautiful Siamese kitten rescued from a garbage dump by Sunkissed Acres NC at just 3.5 months old. She was found with a grievous, wide-open injury to her head.

She had been shot with a pellet-type gun, and the injury went all the way into her scalp. As the result of her severe head wound, she was unable to see or hear until emergency surgery was performed.

Sammie was quickly reserved for adoption thanks to her sweet-as-pie nature, though her adopter had to wait two months for Sammie's wound to heal before welcoming her home. Tragically, shortly after being adopted,

Sammie is truly a lovely little miracle! She has survived being shot as a young kitten and is now recovering from an illness that, until recently, was nearly always fatal.

Sammie became ill and was diagnosed with a historically deadly illness called feline infectious peritonitis, or FIP. Thankfully, there is now an effective (though very costly) treatment that enables FIP kitties to recover. Sammie is currently undergoing this months-long medication regimen and doing well.

Due to the damage caused by her earlier wound, Sammie has been left with a permanent head tilt. It is not painful for her, and we think it only adds to her considerable charm. We are wishing this precious baby continued healing and a lifetime of security, love, and happiness in her forever home!

About the Rescue

Three Brothers Animal Rescue, founded in 2022, is a small, foster-based nonprofit (501[c][3] organization) in Rowan County, North Carolina. The rescue provides homeless and abandoned animals with quality "vetting" (vaccines, spay/neuter, etc.) and care while they are being fostered and readied for adoption.

The group works within the community and with what are termed "kill" shelters in Rowan County to find homes for as many animals as possible. Three Brothers Animal Rescue also focuses on educating the public about spay/neuter programs, to help the stop the mass inflow of unwanted animals.

How to Contact and How to Help

Contact information for Three Brothers Animal Rescue is as follows:

facebook.com/ThreeBrothersAnimalRescue/

instagram.com/ThreeBrothersAnimalRescue/

linktr.ee/threebrothersanimalrescue

tiktok.com/@threebrothersrescue

How to Contact and How to Help, Continued

Three Brothers Animal Rescue posts its adoptable animals on Petfinder. They are viewable at:

https://www.petfinder.com/member/us/nc/salisbury/three-brothers-animal-rescue-nc1210/.

Tax-deductible contributions are always needed and gratefully accepted. Donations may be made as follows:

https://www.paypal.com/paypalme/ThreeBrothersRescue

https://www.venmo.com/threebrothersanimalrescue

Meet Nellie, Nessie, Nora, and Noelle ♥

Tragically, this story is a far too common one. Four orphaned kittens were left to suffer outside in frigid autumn weather but were posted on Facebook for adoption while receiving no care.

When Three Brothers saw the post about the four sisters, who were underage on top of their scary situation, the rescue took action so the babies would not end up meeting a fate worse than their current reality. (Sadly, it is not a rare occurrence for rescues to have to purchase kittens, in such cases, in order to save them.)

The babies were beautiful little calicos but flea and worm infested, with extremely painful ear mites as well. Three Brothers treated the kittens right away, knowing parasites can be deadly to tiny bodies. Once they were healthy, the rescue secured loving forever homes for each and every one of these gorgeous girls!

Clockwise from the top, these precious babies may have met an awful end if not for Three Brothers; frightened at first, the girls are now safe and adored in their forever homes; and finally, Noelle, enjoying the security of her window-only view.

Meet Clora ❤

Clora is the sole survivor of a litter of three kittens found in October 2025 and posted on social media by the finder, who only hoped to secure them good homes. She was persuaded they would be in caring, capable hands with the seemingly kind stranger to whom she gave them. Instead, the kittens were placed in a chicken coop, outside in the cold, and left with no food for several days.

Upon learning of the kittens' devastating plight, Three Brothers took immediate action, convincing the person who now had the babies to surrender them to the rescue. Tragically, the group's valiant efforts came too late for Clora's siblings. Her brother and sister lost their fight in mere hours.

Thankfully, sweet little Clora has managed to overcome her ordeal. Today she is a healthy, almost adoption-ready kitten, thanks to prompt medical attention, safe surroundings, and the good nutrition provided by the rescue and Clora's foster.

It is estimated that 90 percent of kittens born outside do not survive to 6 months of age. Luckily, despite a heartbreaking beginning, Clora is not among those awful statistics. Three Brothers is determined to find this adorable little baby her "happily ever after" in a loving forever home.

Above, Clora's litter. At right, Clora eating her first food in days. Below, Clora as she appears today.

Meet Arby ♥

Arby is an eight-week-old kitten recently saved from a so-called high-kill shelter where she's been for the past ten days. A shelter is a loud and scary place for any cat, let alone a poor little baby all alone!

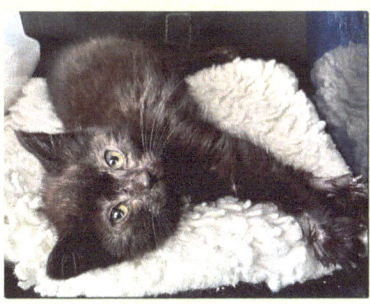

At the shelter Arby developed an upper respiratory infection (URI), essentially a chest cold that is a common occurrence in a stressful environment. Three Brothers rescued Arby from the shelter to help her recover and find a loving forever home.

While Three Brothers has no information on Arby's past, the rescue has quickly discovered that she is a total sweetheart!

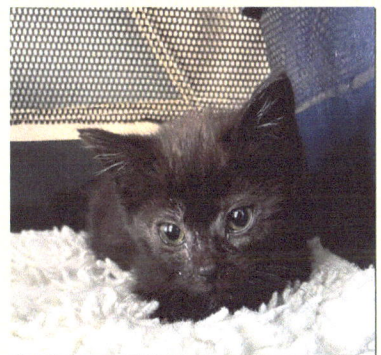

It's a sad fact that black cats are less likely to be adopted than their other-colored counterparts due to superstitious beliefs. It is such an unfortunate truth, as black kittens and cats are often among the friendliest and hardiest of felines.

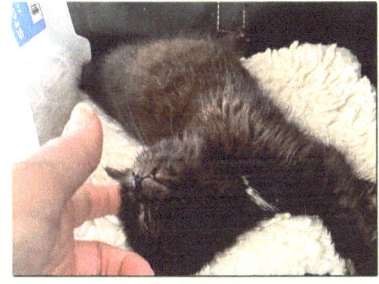

To become the guardian of a beautiful "panther" is among life's great blessings. Therefore, once Arby has recovered from her illness, the rescue is determined to find this little love a bright future and her "happy ever after" in the perfect place!

As the result of malnutrition or illness, a kitten's coat may not initially reflect the rich shade it will ultimately become. Arby's coat will likely darken as she recovers from being sick and continues to mature.

Our Passion and Our Precious Protégés

Our Passion and Our Precious Protégés, Continued

About Mister Mustache Books LLC

Mister Mustache Books is a women-owned small business (a proud organization of two, ha ha) operating in the Charlotte, North Carolina, area. We formed the company in August 2025 when we created our first series of children's books, "The Madcap Mishaps of Mister Mustache." We have since added a second series of children's books to our portfolio called "The Alphabeans" and have a third series, "The Grammarbeans," in the works as well.

We are passionate about creating "Funny Bedtime Stories They'll Love Going to Bed for," lively, entertaining, and always wholesome children's books the whole family will love. We want to grow a new generation of avid readers and book lovers, and we believe humor is a universally enjoyed human condition that will help us get there.

We also believe children and animals make the world a better place. For that reason we donate a share of our proceeds to charitable organizations devoted to helping them. From the time we embarked on our business, we made a conscious decision to integrate charitable giving into everything we do. Not only because it's a good thing to do, but because doing it feels good.

To learn more about us and our children's books, please visit www.mrmustachebooks.com.

Punctuation Rules!™

Hey, Look! The Alphabet Got Funny!™